# SPEAKING IN TONGUES

# TONGUES

## AND

# DIVINE

# HEALING

Robert P. Lightner

REGULAR BAPTIST PRESS
1300 North Meacham Road
P.O. Box 95500
Schaumburg, Illinois 60195

**Library of Congress Cataloging in Publication Data**

Lightner, Robert Paul.
   Speaking in tongues and divine healing.

   Includes bibliographical references.
   1. Glossolalia.  2. Faith-cure.  I. Title.
BL54.L5     248.2    65-5805
ISBN  0-87227-059-9

To Nancy Kay,
Nadine Pearl
and
Natalie Sue—
God's gifts to us

# Contents

# Preface

GOD'S MOST COSTLY GIFT to men was the gift of His Son. The benevolence of God did not terminate at Calvary, however. Through the ministry of the Holy Spirit and on the basis of Calvary, God the Father continues to bestow spiritual gifts upon His own.

This book is written as a testimony that God equips each of His own with abilities to serve Him—with spiritual gifts. It is my firm conviction that some of the gifts of the Spirit were of a temporary nature and that these temporary gifts ceased with the passing of the apostles.

Even though human experiences often seem convincing and hard to understand, they must never determine our faith. Only the Word of God may be trusted as our guide for faith and practice. It is upon this foundation that this study is based.

No attempt has been made to deal with each of the gifts of the Spirit mentioned in the Bible. Rather, I have tried to deal only in a general way with all the gifts and have singled out the gifts of tongues and healing for special attention because of the unusual and widespread interest in them at the present time.

No malice or fun-poking is intended from these

pages. The majority of those who believe in the presence today of what I present as temporary gifts are sincere individuals in love with Jesus Christ. I have no intention of belittling them. On the contrary, I would befriend them, for I share their love for the Savior. Having been involved in the very atmosphere where these temporary gifts were emphasized, I approach the subject with understanding and love for those involved.

It is my earnest prayer that God may be pleased to use these words to bring glory to Jesus Christ.

# ONE

# The Gifts of the Spirit

SERVING THE KING OF KINGS is a royal and noble task requiring supernatural enabling. The Holy Spirit of God provides this divine assistance for every believer, since His requests are always accompanied by divine enabling. The Bible teaches that the Spirit's ministry is as essential for service as it is for salvation. It is as impossible to serve the Lord apart from the Spirit as it is to be saved apart from Him. The Holy Spirit desires to reign in our hearts and to rule in our lives.

It seems that today the Biblical doctrine of the Holy Spirit suffers from three extremes: abuse, neglect and distortion. Some, in all sincerity, overemphasize the truth concerning the Spirit to the extent that other equally important truths are neglected. Others, with equal sincerity and with a desire to guard against undue emotionalism, have so compartmentalized truth concerning the third person of the Godhead that the doctrine is rarely applied to life. Still others, and we are not primarily concerned with their viewpoints here, reject completely the Biblical presentation of the Holy Spirit and thus relegate Him and His ministry to a place of unimportance.

Early councils of the church (Constantinople, A.D.

381, and Chalcedon, A.D. 451) came to clear and lasting decisions regarding the person and work of the Holy Spirit. They based their orthodox viewpoints on the Bible. The problem today, therefore, is not that the conservative doctrinal statements are wrong concerning the Holy Spirit. Rather, we have failed to live in the light of our theology. Our practice in life has not always been consistent with our principles in doctrine. We have all too often been orthodox in doctrine but heretical in practice.

Perhaps the most neglected area of the doctrine of the Holy Spirit has been the ministry of giving gifts to the members of Christ's Body. Lack of understanding regarding spiritual gifts caused a great deal of confusion and disorder in the church at Corinth as it has in many churches since. Perhaps one of the greatest single causes in the church today for splits, disorder, discontentment and the so-called charismatic revival is a failure to understand the ministry of the Holy Spirit in giving gifts.

This study will view the gifts of the Spirit from a fourfold perspective. First of all, the definition of spiritual gifts; second, the distribution and diversity of spiritual gifts; third, the divine purpose of spiritual gifts; and fourth, the divine nature of spiritual gifts.

## DEFINITION OF SPIRITUAL GIFTS

The scriptural testimony regarding spiritual gifts leads to this simple definition: A spiritual gift is "a God-given ability for service."[1] This is a simple definition, but I believe it encompasses all that God would have us know concerning spiritual gifts. Observe the crucial parts of the definition. The ability or enabling comes from God; it is sovereignly bestowed. In 1 Corinthians 12:1 Paul said: "Now concerning spiritual *gifts*. . . ." The word "gifts" is in italics; therefore, it is not in the original language. But the word "spiritual" is, and Paul is really saying, "Now concerning the spiritual faith, brethren, I would not have you ignorant." Thus, gifts are spiritual; they originate with the sovereign Spirit of God.

Again, in 1 Corinthians 12:4 we learn that gifts are related to the grace of God: "Now there are diversities of gifts. . . ." The word for gifts is the word which literally means "grace gifts." Part of the word is the word for grace. So the gifts originate with the Spirit of God, and they are related to the grace of God. Then in verse 7 of the same chapter we read, "But the manifestation of the Spirit is given to every man to profit withal." The word translated *given* helps in defining spiritual gifts. From the usage of this word and from the importance which Paul makes of it, we may say that the source of gifts is spiritual and that their nature is according to grace. Therefore, I repeat the definition: A spiritual gift—whether it is a great gift or a small gift, whether it is the gift of an apostle or the gift of speaking in tongues—is God's enabling to each believer to serve Him.

Spiritual gifts must be distinguished from natural talent. While God may use talents, they are not to be equated with spiritual gifts. Neither are we to consider innate abilities with which we have been born as spiritual gifts. These gifts are not dependent upon education and training. Education does not produce gifts of the Spirit. Academic achievement may help to develop gifts but can never give one a gift since they are given only by God. A spiritual gift is a God-given ability to be used for His service. Furthermore, gifts of the Spirit do not produce spirituality or Christian maturity.

Though it is difficult to determine the exact time when the gifts of the Spirit are given to each individual, it is most reasonable to assume that they are received at the time of salvation when the believer is placed into the Body of Christ by the baptizing work of the Holy Spirit.

This is so because it is at this time that the believer becomes related to the Body of Christ; and the gifts of the Spirit certainly concern our work, our fellowship and our service in the Body of Christ.

No one gets into the Body because of spiritual gifts; but all are equipped with spiritual gifts who are in the Body. The divine purpose of these divine enablings is an exclusive one. They are never to be used to glorify self or even the Holy Spirit. Rather, they are all to be used to glorify Jesus Christ, to display Him and all His excellencies. This the Lord clearly explained in His upper room discourse. His promise to the disciples on those momentous days was that after He departed, the Spirit would come and take up His work, continue it and use it to bring glory to Christ (John 16:13-15).

### DISTRIBUTION AND DIVERSITY OF SPIRITUAL GIFTS

With this definition in mind, let us look at the diversity of gifts and the Spirit's distribution of them. It is very important to remember that the gifts of the Spirit are all based upon the victory of our Lord Jesus Christ at Calvary.

> But unto every one of us is given grace according to the measure of the gift of Christ. Wherefore he saith, When he ascended up on high, he led captivity captive, and gave gifts unto men. (Now that he ascended, what is it but that he also descended first into the lower parts of the earth? He that descended is the same also that ascended up far above all heavens, that he might fill all things.) And he gave some, apostles; and some, prophets; and some, evangelists; and some, pastors and teachers (Eph. 4:7-11).

The reason the Spirit of God can give gifts to men is because of the victory which our Lord achieved at Golgotha. The important thing is not whether that victory was exclusively over Satan, whether it was exclusively over Sheol or Hades, or whether it was over sin and death. The fact is that Jesus Christ became the victor, and as the victor in the battle, He has the sovereign right to bestow the spoils of the battle, spiritual gifts. God the Spirit gives gifts on the basis of Christ's death, and men are thus able to receive them and exercise them on the same basis.

Many kinds of gifts are listed in the New Testament. The three central passages dealing with gifts are 1 Corinthians 12, Romans 12 and Ephesians 4—all written by the apostle Paul. The 1 Corinthians passage provides the longest list of God-given abilities for service. The list is as follows: wisdom, knowledge, faith, healing, miracles, prophecy, discerning of spirits, tongues, interpretation of tongues, the gift of an apostle, teaching, giving assistance or help, and governing (1 Cor. 12:8-28). In Ephesians 4:11 two additional gifts are given—the gift of an evangelist and the gift of a pastor. Still another gift is listed in Romans 12—the gift of liberality. This totals sixteen gifts of the Spirit.

These are not designed necessarily to be exclusive lists of the Spirit's gifts. The emphasis is that whatever God calls men to do, He will also enable men to do. God never calls anyone to do anything without providing the ability to do it. This must be kept in mind. Surely all of these gifts are given to benefit the entire Church of Jesus Christ. Some of them were given to benefit especially the apostolic church, the early church. Others were given to benefit the church throughout all its history. But all of them are given to benefit the entire Church. Every believer—even the most humble, the most illiterate, the youngest—is granted a gift of the Spirit of God.

Some have more than one God-given ability, but every child of God has at least one gift. As this list is observed, it is immediately obvious that all Christians can do some of these things. All can give assistance; all can help; all can give. Every child of God possesses some spiritual gift or gifts, and each one is important to the function of the Body. Paul's entire thrust in 1 Corinthians is that there ought to be diversity in unity and unity in diversity. The Corinthian church had a great problem. In the exercise of these gifts some were being exalted above others. Paul tried to illustrate from the human body that just as every member is important to the proper functioning of the entire system, so every gift, small or great, is necessary to the proper functioning of the Body of Christ.

God gives the gifts to His own and at His own discretion. The "as he will" phrase of 1 Corinthians 12:11 and the "according to his own will" of Hebrews 2:4 both substantiate the divine superintendence in bestowing gifts. Just suppose the choice and distribution of gifts would have been left to men. No doubt all students would choose the gift of wisdom; and all teachers would choose the gift of governing; and most people would want the gift of tongues, since we use our tongues so much. God has not given men this choice, however, and that is obviously a good thing. No, spiritual gifts are gifts *of the Spirit,* to be used *by the Spirit* and *for the glory of Christ.*

Paul's words in 1 Corinthians 12:31 seem to imply that men are to seek and pray for gifts: "But covet earnestly the best gifts: and yet shew I unto you a more excellent way." However, it must be remembered that the apostle was writing to a church which had been infiltrated with individuals who were posing a real problem relative to spiritual gifts. They were exalting minor gifts, and Paul said they were to stop doing that. Covet earnestly the best gifts, he said, and do not emphasize the minor. Speaking to a church which was placing great emphasis on the size of gifts, Paul's argument was that the greater emphasis ought to be placed upon edifying gifts, not gifts that were elementary. It seems quite obvious that the apostle was trying to express that there is a gradation of gifts, that all gifts are not of the same value, and that there is a difference within the gifts. "And God hath set some in the church, first apostles . . ." (1 Cor. 12:28). All gifts were not equal, but all gifts were necessary.

Thus far we have seen what spiritual gifts are. They are divinely bestowed abilities for service. Also, we have seen that the distribution of these gifts is based upon the victory of Christ at Calvary and given as the Spirit wills according to His sovereign choice. Now let us look at the purpose of spiritual gifts.

### DIVINE PURPOSE FOR SPIRITUAL GIFTS

For this we turn to Ephesians 4. Here Paul states very clearly that the purpose for gifts is "for the perfecting of the saints" (Eph. 4:12). Here is one single purpose for God's gifts to men. That one purpose has subordinate purposes, but the first and primary purpose is "for [or unto] the perfecting [the equipping] of the saints." God gives gifts to men so that in turn the church might be equipped, that the Body of Christ might be built up so that there be no schisms in the Body. Gifts are given to effect the growth of the Body, and that means numerical growth as well as spiritual growth. Some of the gifts relate to the spiritual development of the Body of Christ, and other gifts relate to the numerical growth, such as the gift of an evangelist. So both of these aspects are involved in the growth of the Body, and both the spiritual and numerical growth of the Body are to result in glory to Jesus Christ, the Head of the Body.

Some of the gifts which are listed in 1 Corinthians were given as signs to unbelievers. It is clear from 1 Corinthians 14:22 that the gift of tongues was a sign to them that believe not. So while all of the gifts were given for the equipping, the edifying and the building up of the Body of Christ and for His glory, some of them were designed to fulfill that purpose in a different way, as signs to the unbelievers—a verification of the messenger and his message in that day when the canon of Scripture was not yet completed. This divine purpose for spiritual gifts means, therefore, that gifts are never given to exalt or promote self. They are not given to put individuals in the limelight; they are given to magnify and to exalt our Lord Jesus Christ and to build up the Body of Christ.

## DIVINE NATURE OF SPIRITUAL GIFTS

Some of the gifts of the Spirit were given as temporary sign-gifts and are therefore not to be expected in the church today. Does this mean that the Holy Spirit of God is not able to do today what He did in the days of the early church? No, this does not limit the Spirit of God; actually it exalts His sovereignty, for it means that He does not choose to do today what He did in the early church. Some of the gifts are obviously temporary. Everyone who believes the Bible to be the final and complete revelation of God to man must believe that some of the gifts were temporary. For example, one cannot believe that the gift of prophecy or the gift of an apostle is still in operation today and at the same time believe the revelation of God is closed. To believe in the presence of the gift of apostleship today is to believe in apostolic succession. To believe the gift of prophecy is present today is to deny the completeness of the canon of Scripture. By these two gifts at least, the principle of temporary gifts is firmly established. More will be said about these temporary gifts in another chapter.

Summarily, we have sought to deal with the subject of spiritual gifts in a fourfold way. *First*, we defined spiritual gifts as abilities that have been divinely and sovereignly bestowed for service. *Second,* the distribution and diversity of spiritual gifts were presented, and emphasis was placed upon the fact that every believer, every child of God, possesses some spiritual gift. *Third,* the divine purpose in giving gifts was seen to be that of edifying, equipping the Body of Christ for service. *Fourth,* we discovered that some spiritual gifts are permanent and some are temporary.

In conclusion it should be said and clearly understood that the discovery of spiritual gifts in the believer's life is a matter of yieldedness and surrender to the Spirit of God. Paul exhorts in Romans 12:1 that we are to present our bodies as living sacrifices to God. In Romans 6 we are to yield ourselves to the Lord. The same Greek word is translated *yield* in Romans 6 and *present* in Romans 12. Thus, the believer is to present himself to the Holy Spirit of God. This means to disclaim ownership; it means to admit that you are not the boss of your life; it means to surrender to Him and admit that you belong to the Spirit of God. God the Holy Spirit will not reveal His gifts to men apart from the yielded heart and a yielded spirit. Surrender and yieldedness will not produce the gift, but they will awaken one to the reality of the gift and make one conscious of the need to exercise that gift for the glory of Jesus Christ.

NOTE:
1. Charles C. Ryrie, *The Holy Spirit* (Chicago: Moody Press, 1965), p. 83.

# TWO

# Speaking in Tongues

THE PROBLEM WITH the church today is an obvious lack of the manifestation of the power of the Holy Spirit that was so evident in the early days of the church. We have rightfully labored for the protection and preservation of right doctrine concerning the Holy Spirit; but somehow, in spite of this, we have stifled His ministry in our lives and in our churches. Anyone not willing to admit the spiritual dearth and barrenness in our day is either woefully wanting in knowledge or blissfully blinded by Satan into believing that God the Holy Spirit is doing for us and through us all that He wants to do and could do.

What is happening today as a result of dead orthodoxy in the pulpit and spiritual barrenness in the pew has been characteristic of segments of the church throughout its history. Whenever the church has failed to make its message living and livable, there have been those who have reacted by overemphasizing experience. The carnality which characterized the church at Corinth and called forth the rebuke of Paul concerning the misuse and abuse of the gifts of the Holy Spirit has an amazing parallel in many churches today.

In the past few years there has been an amazing upsurge of claims for the revival of what had previously been considered by many as temporary gifts. The gift of tongues has been the gift which has been claimed most. Heretofore expressions of this gift have been confined largely to Pentecostal denominations. That is no longer true. There is a widespread interest today in the reception and exercise of the sign-gifts which were prevalent in the early church.

There have been claims of a resurgence of the gift of tongues in churches, schools and other Christian institutions. Almost every major denomination has been affected; i.e., Episcopalian, Presbyterian, Lutheran, Reformed Church of America and Baptist churches. Schools such as Yale, Fuller Theological Seminary, Wheaton College and Westmont College have had occasions to cope with those who claimed to have the gift of tongues. Such Christian organizations as Inter-Varsity, the Navigators and Wycliffe Bible Translators have also felt ripplings of the tongues tide.

Three things must be taken into consideration in an evaluation of this present phenomenon. *First,* the criterion of judgment must be the Word of God and not the experience or experiences of man either today or in past days. The real issue is not whether I am able to understand or explain the present claims, but what the teaching of the Bible is on the subject. *Second,* whatever is thought or said must be advocated with deep respect to the Holy Spirit. He is God the Holy Spirit and therefore sovereign. *Third,* it is not a matter of what He can or cannot do but a matter of what He has chosen to do.

With these principles in mind, the subject will be approached under a fourfold consideration: the existence of tongues according to the New Testament; the purpose of tongues according to the New Testament; the regulation of the use of tongues according to the New Testament; and the character of tongues according to the New Testament.

## THE EXISTENCE OF TONGUES ACCORDING TO THE NEW TESTAMENT

Everyone who accepts the Bible as the Word of God must believe that men spoke in tongues, that tongues was a gift of the Holy Spirit, and that the gift existed in the early church.

There is ample scriptural evidence for speaking in tongues in the New Testament. Reference to "speaking with tongues" is found in the following passages: Mark 16:17; Acts 2:4; 10:46; 19:6; 1 Corinthians 12:10, 28, 30; 13:1, 8; 14:2-39.

The classification of the references thus becomes very simple. There is only one reference to tongues in the Gospels, three in the Book of Acts and several references in only one of the epistles.

The scarcity of references does not mean the subject is not important nor that these are the only instances in which men spoke in tongues. However, this is the revelation God has been pleased to give, and therefore it is from these that doctrine and conduct with respect to tongues must be established.

For the purposes of this study, only those references to tongues in Acts and 1 Corinthians will be considered. The reference in Mark 16:17 comes in a passage (Mark 16:9-20) which does not appear in the two most ancient manuscripts which we possess. Hence, what is there recorded may very well have happened, but it is doubtful that Mark recorded it. At any rate, even if the reference be included, what is stated in Mark 16:17 in no way contradicts the rest of the New Testament teaching on the subject.

An examination of these passages will confirm the

fact that speaking in tongues actually occurred. It was not an hallucination; neither is it to be explained as the babblings of soothsayers. It was a genuine work of the Holy Spirit of God. It was supernatural and therefore defies any rationalization. This is the only view which harmonizes with the Biblical testimony and does justice to the accuracy of Scripture. The issue is not whether the gift of tongues was real but whether it was temporary or permanent and, therefore, whether it may be expected in the church today.

## THE PURPOSE OF TONGUES
## ACCORDING TO THE NEW TESTAMENT

If the divine purpose for the bestowal of tongues is clearly understood, much will be gained toward an understanding of whether the gift was temporary or permanent. Mr. Zane Hodges has put it succinctly: "It should be clear that the issue of whether miraculous speaking in tongues is a genuine modern-day *charisma* or not will be decided largely by whether or not its Scripturally revealed purpose is likewise a divine purpose for the day in which we live."[1]

The purpose of tongues was of a missionary nature like the other sign-gifts which accompanied the infancy stage of the church. This is not the prejudiced opinion of this writer, but the precise proclamation of the oracles of God. The central passage dealing with the purpose of tongues is 1 Corinthians 14:20-22:

> Brethren, be not children in understanding: howbeit in malice be ye children, but in understanding be men. In the law it is written, With men of other tongues and other lips will I speak unto this people; and yet for all that will they not hear me, saith the Lord. Wherefore tongues are for a sign, not to them that believe, but to them that believe not: but prophesying serveth not for them that believe not, but for them which believe.

The apostle's declaration arose in the context of his rebuke for the carnality and disorder in the exercise of gifts among the Corinthians. According to verse 20, the people were acting childish in their understanding of the gift. Verse 21 constitutes a quotation from Isaiah 28:11 and 12 from which the apostle's conclusion is stated in verse 22: "Wherefore tongues are for a sign, not to them that believe, but to them that believe not." Thus, Paul sees in Isaiah 28:11 and 12 a prophecy of the gift of tongues as a sign to the nation Israel, and it is indeed significant that he relates that prophecy to the Corinthian problem of tongues. He does this to show them the purpose for which the gift was given in the first place and thereby to show them how their misuse had distracted from that divine purpose. The phrase "this people" in verse 21 and in its original setting of Isaiah 28 can only refer to the Jewish nation. Likewise the phrase "them that believe not" or the faithless in verse 22 must be understood as a reference not confined to unsaved Jews but to the unbelieving Jews spoken of in verse 21 as "this people."

This purpose for the gift of tongues, presented so clearly by the apostle Paul, is verified by Luke's three reports of those who spoke in tongues (Acts 2:4; 10:46; 19:6). A study of each of these passages with their contexts will reveal that Jews were present when men spoke in tongues. It is also clear that in each case speaking in tongues was a sign.

Thus the purpose of tongues, according to the Biblical record, was to be a sign to faithless and unbelieving Israel and an authentication of the messenger and the message.

## THE REGULATION OF THE USE OF TONGUES ACCORDING TO THE NEW TESTAMENT

Paul clearly sets forth definite principles to be observed in the use of tongues. These principles are six in number and are given in 1 Corinthians 14:20-40.

**The Principle of Maturity (v. 20).**   After expressing his own desire to be understood when he spoke (v. 19), Paul proceeds to show that to fail in this direction was to be as children—immature (v. 20). Thus, in view of the purpose of the gift, the Corinthians are to act as adults and not to desire the gift for its own merit.

**The Principle of Edification (v. 26).**   It is clear from this verse that each gift and all the gifts combined were to be used as a means of edification and not self-glorification. The exercise of each of the gifts was to build up the Body of Christ, not the one using the gift.

**The Principle of Number and Order (vv. 27, 40).**   If the church services at Corinth were like others in that day, they were three to six hours in length. The principle here is that only two and at the very most three individuals were to speak at one service. Paul adds "and that by course" (v. 27), one after the other, not all at the same time. The principle is further amplified by verse 40: "Let all things be done decently and in order."

**The Principle of Interpretation (v. 27).**   Through some means, perhaps by past experience, the one who wished to experience the gift of tongues was to determine whether someone was present who could interpret before he spoke. If an interpreter was not present, the gift of tongues was not to be exercised (v. 28).

**The Principle of Silence (v. 34).**   If this admonition would be heeded, it would eliminate much of the present tongues movement. Since women are to keep silent in the churches, they evidently did not have the gift. The force of this argument cannot be destroyed by interpreting the word *speak* in verse 34 as anything other than that, since the very same verb is found in verse 28 where it surely means a verbal expression.

**The Principle of Prohibition (v. 39).**     Because of all the warnings which the apostle has sounded regarding tongues, he evidently deemed it necessary to be sure he was not being misunderstood. It is as though he were saying, "I don't mean you should forbid people to speak in tongues." Of course, he was writing to the Corinthians and the gift was then in existence; therefore, those who had the gift were not to be forbidden to exercise it.

## THE CHARACTER OF TONGUES ACCORDING TO THE NEW TESTAMENT

**The Language Character of Tongues.**

*Tongues in Acts.*     An attempt has been made to demonstrate that the *purpose* of tongues was identical in the Acts and 1 Corinthians references. It will now be seen that the *character* or *nature* of tongues is also the same in Acts and 1 Corinthians. The character of tongues may be described as known human languages. It cannot be proved that tongues ever consisted in ecstatic utterances or incomprehensible babblings of gibberish. The Jews in Jerusalem gathered on the Day of Pentecost evidenced the initial tongues experience, and they said: "And how hear we every man in our own tongue, wherein we were born? . . . We do hear them speak in our tongues the wonderful works of God" (Acts 2:8, 11). The miraculous nature of the tongues was not in their incomprehensibility but in the fact that each of those present understood in his own language, evidently without an interpreter, what the disciples were preaching in their own language.

The Holy Spirit of God did miraculously on the Day

of Pentecost what it has taken modern science almost two millennia to mimic mechanically. Today at United Nations meetings a speaker speaks in his native tongue and, by means of mechanical devices which interpret his speech, he is understood by delegates who can neither speak nor understand the speaker's tongue.

This known human language character of tongues may also be illustrated from the other occurrences of tongues in Acts. Peter reviews the happenings of Acts 10 in chapter 11. His explanation clearly links what happened at Caesarea when the Holy Spirit came with what happened at Jerusalem when the Spirit came. He says: ". . . The Holy Ghost fell on them, as on us at the beginning" (Acts 11:15). Dr. Walvoord's comment summarizes the argument: "By the express statement of Acts 11:15 the phenomenon of speaking in tongues in Caesarea was similar to the experience at Pentecost. If these two instances are essentially the same, Acts 19 would follow. It would be, certainly, arbitrary and strained exegesis to make a distinction when none is made in the text."[2] It is clear from the contexts of each of the Acts references that the tongues spoken were known languages, though not necessarily known to the speaker.

*Tongues in 1 Corinthians.*   It remains to be shown that the references to tongues in 1 Corinthians are also to known human languages and not ecstatic utterances. It is often argued that while known foreign languages may have been involved in Acts, the tongues in 1 Corinthians were ecstatic or heavenly vocalizations. Support for this view usually comes from the frequent appearance of the word *unknown* in 1 Corinthians 14. Argument is also often based on the references to "tongues of angels" in 13:1; speaking to God in a tongue, 14:2; and to spirit praying in a tongue, 14:14.

By answering these objections and by presenting other positive reasons, it will be demonstrated that the gift is the same in 1 Corinthians as in Acts.

The argument from the appearance of the word *unknown* in chapter 14 is the weakest of all. The word *unknown* in each case is italicized in the Authorized Version, thus indicating its omission in the original. This word was added for clarification, but its addition has only produced confusion.

The expression "tongues of men and of angels" in 13:1 appears in a section where Paul is making extreme contrasts in order to exalt the necessity of love. He does not mean to imply that he actually excelled in the qualities he lists. He merely is seeking to show the necessary supremacy of love. He no more expects the Corinthians to speak angelic languages than he expects them to torture their bodies by burning them (v. 3).[3]

In 14:2 and 14, the apostle is seeking to communicate the fact that those who speak in a tongue not known to the hearer speak without human understanding; thus the need for an interpreter (1 Cor. 14:5, 27). In verse 2 the one who speaks in a tongue not known to the hearer speaks only to God. The same fact is true in verse 14. If a person prays in a tongue not known to him, he himself is without understanding. Neither of these passages or the one in 13:1 presents any substantial argument opposing the fact that these were foreign languages.

In addition to the arguments listed above which militate against making tongues in 1 Corinthians anything other than known languages, there are definite positive reasons for making them identical with those in Acts—the miraculous use of foreign languages for the verification of the gospel.

*First,* if *glossa* (tongues) in all its forms means tongues in Acts, there is no reason to change the translation in 1

Corinthians. Actually, the word *language* might be substituted for every occurrence of the word *tongue* or *unknown tongue*. In addition to this fact, no qualifying words are used in 1 Corinthians to distinguish those tongues and those in Acts. This use of identical terms provides no grammatical or exegetical basis for making the distinction so often made.

*Second,* Paul's argument of the utter uselessness of tongues unless they are understood is a strong argument in favor of saying they are the same.

> Now, brethren, if I come unto you speaking with tongues, what shall I profit you, except I shall speak to you either by revelation, or by knowledge, or by prophesying, or by doctrine? And even things without life giving sound, whether pipe or harp, except they give a distinction in the sounds, how shall it be known what is piped or harped? For if the trumpet give an uncertain sound, who shall prepare himself to the battle? So likewise ye, except ye utter by the tongue words easy to be understood, how shall it be known what is spoken? for ye shall speak into the air (1 Cor. 14:6-9).

*Third,* the city of Corinth was thriving with commercial affairs and was, no doubt, inhabited by Jews of numerous linguistic backgrounds. Thus many languages were present which were unknown to the Greeks. Therefore, the miraculous use of this sign-gift at Corinth was as necessary as it was in Jerusalem (Acts 2), Caesarea (Acts 10) or Ephesus (Acts 19).

*Fourth,* in contrast to a single ecstatic utterance, there are said to be different kinds of tongues or languages (1 Cor. 12:10). Along this same line, if tongues are not foreign languages, it is difficult to see how they can be a sign to the faithless (1 Cor. 14:22). Too, Paul refers to "many kinds of voices" of which he evidently knew many

(1 Cor. 14:10; cf. 14:18) and used to good advantage in his missionary work.

*Summary.*      Thus, the gift of tongues in the New Testament does not involve two different kinds of tongues—one consisting of known foreign languages (Acts 2, 10, 19) and the other of ecstatic utterances (1 Cor. 12—14). Rather, all references relate to the miraculous ability to speak known and recognizable foreign languages. This is not to say there were no attempts to counterfeit the miraculous. Perhaps such very attempts gave rise to Paul's harsh rebuke concerning them. Unquestionably those who possessed the natural ability to use foreign languages often used them in the assembly as a demonstration of their ability and not as a gift. Perhaps still others who could only speak one language and did not possess the gift attempted to imitate those who did, and this surely produced vain gibberish babblings.

From the above it ought to be clear what speaking in tongues was. It might also be profitable to state briefly what it was not. It was not identical with the baptism of the Holy Spirit; neither did all who were baptized speak in tongues (1 Cor. 12:13, 30). This fact also proves that the gift was not a test of salvation. Much of the present confusion relating to the baptism of the Spirit and tongues exists because of the failure to distinguish between the baptizing and the filling ministry of the Spirit. Judging from the carnality present in the church at Corinth, speaking in tongues was certainly not an evidence of spirituality (1 Cor. 3:1). The Scriptures know nothing of seeking for the baptism of the Spirit. No one was ever exhorted to seek this ministry of the Spirit. There is exhortation to seek the filling of the Spirit (Eph. 5:18), that is, to seek His control of one's life. The baptism of the Spirit is the Holy Spirit's work of placing the believing sinner into the Body of Christ (1 Cor. 12:13) and the sphere of the resurrected life of Christ (Rom. 6:1-10). He is the instrument that places one into that sphere of blessing.

**The Limited Character of Tongues.**    There are several reasons for believing that the gift of tongues was a temporary gift which was limited by the sovereign God to only a few individuals in the apostolic church and only to the apostolic church.

*1. The silence regarding the gift.*    It is indeed significant that most of the New Testament writers are silent concerning tongues. As has been indicated earlier, reference to tongues appears certainly in only two books of the New Testament. The other books of the New Testament do not even so much as refer to the phenomenon. The validity of arguments from silence is often questionable. However, in this case it is not mere silence but loud silence. This argument would be of little significant value except for the fact that these other books, in which speaking in tongues is not mentioned, devote a great deal of attention to the doctrine of the Holy Spirit. Thus, we would expect the writers to include something somewhere about tongues if it is a corollary of the Spirit's ministry, universal among all who have been baptized by Him.

*2. The purpose of the gift.*    The sign-significant purpose of the gift has already been established. The scriptural testimony bears sufficient witness to the fact that the ability to speak in other tongues (languages) vindicated and authenticated both the messenger and his message to the nation Israel (1 Cor. 14:21, 22; cf. Isa. 28:11, 12). Since God is not now dealing with Israel as a nation but has allowed the nation to be scattered and taken captive into all nations (Matt. 23:37-39; Luke 21:20-24), it should be self-evident that the purpose for which the gift was given is no longer present, and thus the presence of the gift need not be expected.

*3. The principle of temporary gifts.* To deny that some gifts are temporary is to deny the finality and completeness of the Word of God. For example, if the gift of an apostle is still available today, there must still be those who possess the qualifications for that office. Romanism insists on the presence of this gift in its doctrine of apostolic succession. C. I. Scofield lists the scriptural qualifications, the most important of which is the necessity of being an eyewitness of the Resurrection (Acts 1:22; 1 Cor. 9:1).[4] That apostleship was a gift is clearly indicated by its inclusion with other gifts (Eph. 4:11; 1 Cor. 12:28). It is also listed as the most important of all gifts (1 Cor. 12:28) and the foundation upon which the superstructure is built (Eph. 2:20). If the most important gift is no longer present but passed with the first generation of Christians, it is certainly reasonable to assume that the least of all gifts—tongues—has also ceased (1 Cor. 12:10, 28).

Likewise, the gift of prophecy has ceased. Failure to accept this fact paved the way for millennial Dawnism and the religion of Father Divine. It must be acknowledged that there are two aspects to this gift. One relates to foretelling and the other to forthtelling. The forthtelling aspect is still present and is exercised by preachers, but the foretelling aspect is not. Since the Spirit of God makes a distinction between the gift of prophecy and the gift of pastor-teacher, it must be assumed that He is speaking of prophecy in the foretelling sense. The gift is mentioned in 1 Corinthians 12:10, 28; 14:1-40 and Romans 12:6. It is classed second in importance (1 Cor. 12:28). A prophet in this special sense is one who received a special revelation from God and whose message had the divine authority of

God. If this gift is still in operation, the canon of Scripture is not closed, Hebrews 1:1 is a farce, and we may expect new messages from God in addition to the Word of God.

There are other temporary gifts such as miracles and healing, but enough has been said to establish the principle of temporary gifts and thus allow for the temporary nature of tongues.

4. *The testimony of Scripture.*    Two passages of Scripture deal specifically with the cessation of the gift of tongues. The first of these is 1 Corinthians 13:8. That tongues would cease is plainly taught in this verse. "Charity never faileth: but whether there be prophecies, they shall fail; whether there be tongues, they shall cease; whether there be knowledge, it shall vanish away." This passage must be understood in its setting. Chapters 12 through 14 of 1 Corinthians deal with the existence and exercise of spiritual gifts. Chapter 12 relates to the problem of spiritual gifts in the Corinthian church. Chapter 13 is concerned with the supremacy and necessity of the practice of love in the exercise of gifts. Chapter 14 deals with the practical application of the principles of love in the use of the gifts.

The contrast is made in chapter 13 that love is more important than any of the gifts because it is eternal. The thesis is, "Charity [love] never faileth" (1 Cor. 13:8). The temporal and temporary are clearly related to the enduring and eternal in verse 10. The gifts of prophecy, tongues and knowledge mentioned in 13:8-10 are temporary; love is eternal. The problem is, What is the force of the future tenses? Some say they refer to the completion of the canon; others apply them to the coming of the Lord. That the future tenses of verse 8 refer to the close of the canon, or that time when God's revelation has been all recorded, is strongly implied for the following reasons.

*First*, Paul states that these gifts were partial, and thus he implies their replacement by the full or complete (1 Cor. 13:9, 10). Both knowledge and prophecy as gifts were exercised out of a portion (v. 9), that is, a portion of revelation because the New Testament canon was not yet complete.

*Second*, the word *perfect* (v. 10) in order to refer to Christ and His coming ought to be in the masculine gender, but it is not; it is in the neuter gender.

*Third*, from verse 11 it is clearly indicated there will be a certain course followed from the infancy stage of the church to the mature stage. Paul's illustration reminds one not to expect habits of infancy to be present in one who is mature. Likewise, the gift of tongues was suited to the infancy stage to authenticate the message, but was no longer needed when the totality of God's truth had been revealed, just as baby habits are not expected in manhood (1 Cor. 13:11).

Since knowledge is listed with the other gifts, it must so be classified. It refers to unusual spiritual insight and may be closely associated with the gift of discerning spirits (1 Cor. 12:10). Certainly prophecy is a temporary gift and has ceased, else the canon is not complete and we do not have all of God's Word.

Some have proposed since the same verb, *katargeo,* is used for the termination of prophecies and knowledge and an entirely different verb, *pauo,* with reference to tongues, that thereby Paul is teaching that prophecy and knowledge will cease at the Rapture, and tongues have ceased with the apostolic church.[5] There is much to commend this view. From this argument and the one presented above, there is solid exegetical basis for the termination of tongues with the early church.

A second passage is Hebrews 2:3 and 4. The writer says, "How shall we escape, if we neglect so great salvation; which at the first began to be spoken by the Lord, and was confirmed unto us by them that heard him; God also bearing them witness, both with signs and wonders, and with divers miracles, and gifts of the Holy Ghost, according to his own will?"

Conservative scholarship is usually agreed in placing the date of Hebrews somewhere between A.D. 65 to 69. Thus the book is addressed to second generation Christians, the point being that Christians of the first generation experienced some things even the second generation Christians did not. While the gift of tongues is not specifically mentioned, signs and sign-gifts are. Evidently by the time of the writing these had already passed from the earthly scene. The passage is conclusive proof of the limited and temporary nature of some gifts, and we believe the gift of tongues must be included among them. To believe that attesting gifts, such as the gift of tongues, are still necessary is not only to deny the finality of the written Word but also to deny the climactic attestation of the Living Word (Heb. 1:1).

## SUMMARY AND CONCLUSION

Has the New Testament gift of tongues ceased? That is the burning issue. There are several very strong reasons for believing that the gift ceased when the canon of Scripture was closed.[6]

*First*, the gift ceased historically. History verifies this.

*Second*, the gift of tongues is mentioned definitely in only two books of the New Testament—Acts and 1 Corinthians. The Mark 16 reference comes in a section not included in the oldest Greek manuscripts. Of course, one scriptural statement is enough to establish a teaching; but two things are peculiarly different about the tongues references.

In the first place, the gift of tongues is included in the

list of spiritual gifts only in 1 Corinthians 12. The other two lists of gifts (Rom. 12; Eph. 4) do not include it. This is significant, especially since 1 Corinthians is the earliest of the three books. Does this not at least imply the gift was not in existence when Romans and Ephesians were written?

The second significant thing about the scarcity of scriptural support is that the doctrine of the Holy Spirit's person and work is taught extensively in New Testament books not mentioning the gift of tongues.

*Third,* tongues was a sign-gift especially for the nation Israel. The ability to speak in a language which was not learned authenticated the apostles and their message; therefore, it was limited to the apostolic age.

*Fourth,* sign-gifts were given only through the apostles. There is no scriptural evidence that these gifts—tongues among them—were ever received apart from apostolic ministry. It follows that when the apostles died, so did the gift.

*Fifth,* some gifts were temporary. If this is not granted, it cannot be said that the canon of Scripture is closed. Surely the gifts of predictive prophecy and of apostle have ceased. The Roman Catholic Church teaches apostolic succession and believes the gift of apostle is still present. Some who believe the New Testament gift of tongues is still operative are consistent enough to say that the gift of apostle is still present. An example of this is the Irvingites who call themselves the Catholic Apostolic Church.

*Sixth,* Paul states that tongues would cease completely (1 Cor. 13:8). The gifts of prophecy and knowledge are also listed. These three gifts are said to be temporary; love is eternal. The future in the passage "shall cease" refers to that time when the canon of Scripture would be complete.

*Seventh,* sign-gifts were not present among second generation Christians. The writer of Hebrews makes this clear (Heb. 2:3, 4). Hebrews was written to second generation Christians—A.D. 65-69. By that time the "signs," "wonders" and "divers miracles, and gifts of the Holy Ghost" were no longer present.

If the gift of tongues has ceased, how are the present-day claims of speaking in tongues to be explained? How are we to account for the spiritual benefits people claim to receive from the gift?

In answer to this last question, several things may be said. Most Christians who seek the gift do so by earnestly seeking the Lord's blessing on them in prayer. Many who either speak in a tongue—or want to—honestly desire to be Spirit-filled.

Many seek this gift because they long for some subjective, emotional experience to validate their Christian experience.

The present claims for speaking in tongues can be accounted for in several ways. Since tongues speaking has occurred and still occurs among non-Christians and in pagan religions as well as among Christians, it may be the result of Satanic or demonic influence. Speaking in tongues occurs even among heathen people.

Today speaking in tongues may also be the result of psychological suggestion or psychosomatic manifestations. Tongue advocates often teach their devotees how to begin speaking in tongues. Some Christian psychiatrists are convinced the present-day tongue speaking is altogether psychological.

Not everything which strikes of the miraculous or supernatural is of God. There is evil supernatural power. Pharaoh's magicians had great power (Exod. 7:11, 22; 8:7). Deception and counterfeit are predicted for the last days (Matt. 7:22, 23).

We need to study thoroughly the person and work of the Holy Spirit. It is my conviction that the problems associated with the recent upsurge of tongues and other sign-gifts stem from a failure to understand the person and work of the Holy Spirit in relation to the believer.

Our greatest need is not to desire to speak in tongues but to use the one tongue God has given us for His glory. Our prayer ought never to be, "Oh, for a thousand tongues," until we have used the one God has given us to the very best of our ability for His glory.

NOTES:
1. Zane C. Hodges, "The Purpose of Tongues," *Bibliotheca Sacra* (July—September, 1963), p. 226.
2. John F. Walvoord, *The Holy Spirit* (Grand Rapids: Zondervan, 1958), p. 183.
3. Hodges, "The Purpose of Tongues," p. 231, footnote.
4. *Scofield Reference Bible,* 1917 Edition, p. 1008, note 1.
5. Stanley D. Toussaint, "First Corinthians Thirteen and the Tongues Question," *Bibliotheca Sacra* (October—December, 1963), pp. 312-316.
6. The material in this section is from Robert P. Lightner, "The Charismatic Movement," *Vital Issues of the Hour in the Light of God's Word* (Schaumburg, IL: Regular Baptist Press, 1973), pp. 42-46.

# THREE

# Divine Healing and Healers

GOD HAS HEALED men of physical infirmities in the past, and He does heal today. That there are divine healers or those who possess the gift of healing today is an entirely different matter, and one which is contrary to God's Word.

Christ died on the cross for our sins, not for our sicknesses. Of course, every benefit and blessing which the child of God receives are given by God on the merits of Christ's work on the cross. This does not mean, however, that it is always God's will for His children to be physically well. Deliverance from the curse and penalty of sin comes the moment the guilty sinner believes. Every other provision of Calvary is from that moment a divine guarantee, though they are not all received at that time. Ultimate and final deliverance from the presence of sin and physical suffering will come when we are transformed into His likeness.

There has been an increased emphasis upon the gift of healing in recent years. Masses of people are gathering in many places to witness and partake in healing campaigns. Men and women are claiming to possess the gift of healing and thus to be divine healers. They are calling

for a return to the days of our Lord by claims of the miraculous which have only been equaled by Christ Himself.

## PHYSICAL HEALING AND THE DEATH OF CHRIST

Why did Christ die? Divine healers answer that He
not only died for the sins of men but also for the sicknesses of men. The only way to arrive at a true answer to this
question is to ask another one: What saith the Scripture?
It makes very little difference what men may say. The
question is, What does the Word of God teach?

**The Possibility of Healing.**    No true believer in the
Bible as the authoritative Word of God could deny that
God's power extends to His ability to heal the physical
body as well as it extends to every other area. God is
omnipotent. The issue then is not, *Can* God heal? Of
course He can, and He does. Rather, the issue is, Does the
death of Christ guarantee the complete and present deliverance from all physical infirmities as it does the complete and present deliverance from the penalty of sin for
those who receive it?

**The Purpose of Christ's Death.**    One unmistakable
purpose in the death of Christ runs throughout the Bible.
Whether it be in prophetic utterances or in the words of
Christ and His disciples, the immediate purpose of the
death of Christ was for the sins of the world. From the
simplest to the most profound passage of Scripture, the
death of Christ is related to man's sin. It was because of
the sin of Adam and our participation in it that Jesus
Christ came to die on the cross. The words of Luke 19:10
sum up the Bible-revealed purpose of the death of Christ:
"For the Son of man is come to seek and to save that
which was lost" (Luke 19:10).

The Savior did minister to the physical needs of men.

The Gospel records bear abundant testimony to this. However, His earthly ministry did not have as its primary and culminative objective the curing of physical ills. He came not to heal the sick but to save the lost.

The blood of Christ is never referred to as a sickness cure but as a sin cure. First John 1:7 tells us, "The blood of Jesus Christ his Son cleanseth us from all sin." It does not say that the blood cleanseth us from all sickness. Our sins are repeatedly referred to as having been borne by Him on the cross. Paul's testimony is that God the Father made God the Son to be sin for us, not sickness for us (2 Cor. 5:21).

*1. The testimony of prophecy.* Only an unbelieving heart would deny that Psalm 22 anticipates the death of Christ. Primarily, the conversation is between God the Father and God the Son. The very words that the unbelieving crucifiers would say and the means by which they would kill Him are all in this Psalm. Is it not strange that David would anticipate all the details of Christ's death and omit bodily healing in connection with it? Throughout this entire Psalm there is not one hint that bodily healing is in the atonement. As a matter of fact, no area of bodily healing is touched upon in this glorious anticipation of the provision of Jesus Christ.

In direct contrast to the claim of divine healers, Isaiah 53:5 does not teach healing in the atonement. There is absolutely nothing in the text or context to warrant such a claim. When Isaiah says, "and with his stripes we are healed" (Isa. 53:5), he is simply summing up what he previously said, namely, that Jesus Christ was wounded and bruised for our sin.

Not only do the prophecies concerning the death of Christ (and there are many more than here stated) fail to deal with the matter of bodily healing, but the types of

His death fail to do so as well. Not one of these types of His death, and there are at least sixteen, reveals anything about bodily healing, either in its primary meaning or in the type it represents.

There was nothing about bodily healing in the offerings or sacrifices of the Old Testament, of which Christ became the perfect offering. They all deal with the remission of sin, not sickness. Why did these Old Testament saints not know anything about physical healing in the coming redemption?

2. *The testimony of the Savior.*    Matthew 28:19 says, "Go ye therefore, and teach all nations, baptizing them in the name of the Father, and of the Son, and of the Holy Ghost." These words constitute the final gospel-preaching command of the Lord Jesus Christ. No mention is made in this command of any healing or sign-gifts as Matthew penned it. He was writing to Jews who knew about the promised Messiah and had even witnessed many of the miracles performed by the Twelve, the Seventy and Christ Himself. And yet, He excludes all about physical healing and commands them to teach and baptize instead.

When speaking about His departure and the coming of the Holy Spirit Jesus said, "And when he is come, he will reprove the world of sin, and of righteousness, and of judgment" (John 16:8). Again this passage is void of any command to heal. The Holy Spirit's ministry is to reprove the world of sin and of righteousness and of judgment, not to rid the world of physical ills. Both of these passages (Matt. 28:19 and John 16:8) take us to a very strategic point in Christ's ministry. He was about to leave His disciples. If there was ever a time when they needed direction, it was at this time. They had been depending upon Him, possibly too much, and now He was going to go away, and they were about to walk alone. Their last command from their Captain did not include anything about physical healing. Christ did not command His disciples to heal as part of God's salvation-gospel. Rather, He commanded them to love one another, which was an evidence of their love for God. He said, "These things I command you, that ye love one another" (John 15:17).

The words of the Lord Himself reveal His true purpose in His coming: "I am come that they might have life, and that they might have it more abundantly" (John 10:10). Notice He did not say that He came in order that men need not suffer anymore. He in no way implies that He came to die for the physical ailments which our bodies encounter. When Christ instituted the Lord's Supper, He told His disciples to drink the wine which was a symbol of His shed blood; and He said, "Drink ye all of it; For this is my blood of the new testament, which is shed for many for the remission of sins" (Matt. 26:27, 28).

3. *The testimony of Paul.* When the rulers of the synagogue gave Paul opportunity to speak for himself, he very plainly explained the purpose of the death of Christ: "Be it known unto you therefore, men and brethren, that through this man is preached unto you the forgiveness of sins: And by him all that believe are justified from all things, from which ye could not be justified by the law of Moses" (Acts 13:38, 39). In the presence of this company of Jews, including the rulers of the synagogue, when Paul speaks of the death and resurrection of Christ he says nothing about physical healing. His emphasis is upon the forgiveness of sin through the blood of Christ.

Again in Romans 4:25 Paul speaks with clarity about the death of Christ when he says that Christ "was delivered for our offences, and was raised again for our justification." Christ did not die because of or for our sicknesses but on account of and for our sin. His vicarious and sub-stitutionary death was for sin, not sickness.

First Corinthians 15:1-4 is generally referred to as the definition of the gospel; as such, it is known to practically every child of God. In this simple declaration of what the gospel is, Paul states: "Christ died for our sins according to the scriptures" (1 Cor. 15:3). Paul never taught that Christ died and shed His blood to take away our diseases. The testimony of the prophets, of Christ, of Paul and of every other Biblical writer was, in effect, simply this: The Son of God became the Son of Man and died in order that the sons of men might become the sons of God.

Many are the accomplishments of Christ in His death. In addition to becoming a substitute for sin, He ended the Mosaic law; provided redemption, reconcili-ation, propitiation; judged the sin nature; and provided the basis for the believer's forgiveness. Many other things could be added to the list. Scripture never guarantees present deliverance from physical sickness as one of the immediate benefits of Calvary.

## PHYSICAL HEALING AND THE WILL OF GOD

Divine healers make bold and dogmatic claims that it is always God's will to heal. Those who believe this at-tempt to prove their point in various ways. Of course, the basis for the idea that it is always God's will to heal springs from another error, which is that physical healing was provided for in the death of Christ. Very obviously, if Christ died for our sicknesses and if healing for the body is as sure as healing for the soul, then of course it is God's will always to heal our bodies. In other words, the prem-ise is false. Christ did not die to give us present freedom from sicknesses; therefore, it is not always God's will to heal the bodies of all His children.

In spite of the repeated claims of exponents of this

theory, hundreds, yes thousands, of men and women of God have prayed in all faith and sincerity and have not been healed. If it is always God's will to heal and if concern in regard to His will is wrong, why have not all of God's children been cured when they have prayed? The power of God is not the problem. God has all power. He is able to do exceeding and abundantly above all we ask or think. The problem is rather this: Is what I am asking of God His will for me at this moment? This matter of praying in connection with the will of God is very scriptural.

The apostle Paul serves as a good example of one who became obedient to the will of God. Paul had been caught up into heaven and lest he should become exalted above measure the Lord sent to him a "thorn in the flesh." The nature of the "thorn" will not be discussed here. The important thing to keep in mind is that it was "in his flesh." In other words, it was something physical. It was not a mental or spiritual problem; it was physical. Paul's prayer was not answered by the removal of the physical affliction. Instead, God gave him grace sufficient for his need to triumph in spite of the infirmity. Instead of accusing God for his problem, he gloried in his infirmity, knowing it was the will of God (2 Cor. 12:9).

Epaphroditus serves as another witness to the fact that it is not always God's will to heal the body. In Philippians 2:25-30 he is described as a devoted servant of the Lord. To Paul he was a fellow laborer and companion in the gospel. However, there was one thing which marked him; he was very sick. In fact, he was near death. The word of his illness spread from Rome to Philippi. Many saints prayed for him, including Paul himself. The Scriptures do not say that a healer came and laid his hands on him or that he was rebuked for his lack of faith. He was sick for a long time and prayers remained unanswered until it was God's will to heal him. Then, and only then, was Epaphroditus healed. It was not God's will to heal him at first. God does not reveal why this was the case; He simply allowed him to be sick, in spite of the great apostle's prayers, until in His own good time and way He healed him.

Another Biblical example of the will of God in bodily healing may be given along this same line. Paul esteemed him highly as a preacher. He was a pastor who loved the Lord and had a deep concern for his people as well. But Timothy had stomach trouble. Probably the over-kindness of some of his people or the varying climate and unhealthy water caused this sickness. The inspired advice is, "Drink no longer water, but use a little wine for thy stomach's sake and thine often infirmities" (1 Tim. 5:23). Paul had healed many by the laying on of hands and now he tells Timothy not to claim deliverance because of Calvary, but to use a natural means to effect a stomach cure.

When Paul went on his second missionary journey to Troas, a man by the name of Trophimus was with him (Acts 20:4). Paul had this to say about him: "Trophimus have I left at Miletum sick" (2 Tim. 4:20). Evidently Trophimus was a close companion of Paul, and yet he was sick. In fact, he was so sick that Paul left him at Miletum to remain quiet. Paul, the great Christian warrior who had healed with the laying on of hands, did not tell Trophimus to appropriate the death and resurrection of Christ. This man was born again and yet sick.

A day is coming when Jesus Christ shall transform these bodies of our humiliation to the likeness of His glorious body, but that day is still in the future. Until that day there needs to be a submission to the sovereign will of Almighty God.

## MISINTERPRETED PASSAGES REFUTED

In order to have a basis for the present-day doctrine

of healing, various passages of Scripture are used. These passages are used to prove not only divine healing but all of the associate beliefs connected with it as well.

### Isaiah 53:4-6

> Surely he hath borne our griefs, and carried our sorrows: yet we did esteem him stricken, smitten of God, and afflicted. But he was wounded for our transgressions, he was bruised for our iniquities: the chastisement of our peace was upon him; and with his stripes we are healed. All we like sheep have gone astray; we have turned every one to his own way; and the LORD hath laid on him the iniquity of us all.

In this crucial passage the prophet speaks of the Messiah's ministry in relation to physical healing (v. 4) and in relation to spiritual healing (vv. 5, 6).

According to Matthew the Lord fulfilled the first part of verse 4 of Isaiah's prophecy during His earthly ministry as He cast out demons and healed all that were sick (Matt. 8:17). The assurance of this comes from the obvious fact that what our Lord was doing according to the record of Matthew 8 took place long before the cross. Since Isaiah 53:4 is related to the casting out of evil spirits and the healing of all that were sick *before the cross,* there is no support here for physical healing in the atonement.

It is rather common knowledge that the word translated *healed* is not limited in its meaning to physical healing. "In Luke 4:18 it refers to the alleviation of heartaches, and in Hebrews 12:13, to the rectifying of one's conduct. In Matthew 13:15, it means, 'to bring about (one's) salvation.' "[1]

Even though Peter does not claim to be quoting Isaiah, there seems to be a relationship between his statement in 1 Peter 2:24 and Isaiah's in 53:5. The central idea in Peter's statement is He "bare our sins." Likewise, the heart of Isaiah's message is, "He was wounded for our transgressions, he was bruised for our iniquities." This being true, one must also interpret the "healing" in each passage as spiritual and not physical.

In summary, then, Isaiah prophesied of the life sufferings of Christ through which He sympathetically identified Himself with our physical infirmities and sicknesses (Isa. 53:4; Matt. 8:17). Also, he prophesied of the sufferings of Christ in death through which, according to the prophet's own words and the words of the apostle Peter, He made provision for our spiritual sicknesses (Isa. 53:4-6; 1 Pet. 2:24).

Our Lord's identification with our physical griefs and sorrows was in His life; and His identification with our transgressions and iniquities was in His death when He was stricken and smitten of God.

## Psalm 103:1-8

> Bless the LORD, O my soul: and all that is within me, bless his holy name. Bless the LORD, O my soul, and forget not all his benefits: Who forgiveth all thine iniquities; who healeth all thy diseases; Who redeemeth thy life from destruction; who crowneth thee with lovingkindness and tender mercies; Who satisfieth thy mouth with good things; so that thy youth is renewed like the eagle's. The LORD executeth righteousness and judgment for all that are oppressed. He made known his ways unto Moses, his acts unto the children of Israel. The LORD is merciful and gracious, slow to anger, and plenteous in mercy.

The third verse of this passage has probably been used to prove healing in the atonement more than any other verse in the Bible. The *all* is said to mean that God will heal all our diseases. We may ask, What of the fifth verse: "Thy youth is renewed like the eagle's"? If the healing of all diseases refers to the present age, so does this promise in verse five of renewed youth for the aged.

If immediate physical healing has been provided for in the death of Christ, then that healing must of necessity be just as eternal as the spiritual healing provided for in His death. The death of Christ dealt with eternal issues. His death made possible eternal life to as many as believe. If physical healing was also provided for in that death, it too must be eternal. In other words, in the same sense in which the believing sinner receives pardon from sin forever by believing the gospel, so at the same instant that sinner should receive deliverance from physical sickness forever. Why should there be a different time, progressive or otherwise, when physical deliverance is achieved?

## James 5:10-15

> Take, my brethren, the prophets, who have spoken in the name of the Lord, for an example of suffering affliction, and of patience. Behold, we count them happy which endure. Ye have heard of the patience of Job, and have seen the end of the Lord; that the Lord is very pitiful, and of tender mercy. But above all things, my brethren, swear not, neither by heaven, neither by the earth, neither by any other oath: but let your yea be yea; and your nay, nay; lest ye fall into condemnation. Is any among you afflicted? let him pray. Is any merry? let him sing psalms. Is any sick among you? let him call for the elders of the church; and let them pray over him, anointing him with oil in the name of the Lord: And the prayer of faith shall save the sick, and the Lord shall raise him up; and if he have committed sins, they shall be forgiven him.

There are two underlying and important phrases in this passage: "the prayer of faith" and "anointing him with oil in the name of the Lord," the most important one being "the prayer of faith." This becomes the issue of the entire passage. What this prayer is, when it is to be prayed, and by whom it is to be prayed are matters which cause division. This section in the Book of James is quoted very frequently to prove that it is always God's will to heal the Christian. To prove this point emphasis is laid upon the word "shall." In spite of the healers' claims, thousands of prayers have been offered, even by the healers, that have not been answered.

The question may legitimately be asked, Who has this prayer of faith? If this is an ordinance for the local church today, as some healers claim, some explanation must be given why godly men and women pray in all faith and their prayers are not always answered in regard to physical healing. Then, too, the divine healers fail to realize that James refers his sick patients to the "elders." In fact, the sick one is to call for the elders. The elders are not to seek out the sick (v. 14). The praying and anointing are to be done within the limits of the local church. This does not prove, by any means, that anointing and praying are local church ordinances as water baptism and the Lord's Supper. Not everything the elders, or overseers, did was a church ordinance. But this does prove that those who were sick were to go to or call on their pastor to anoint and pray for them, not some healer who neither represented nor ministered from the local church.

If it is God's will for everyone to be physically well, the prophets which James mentions were out of God's will. James gives these as an example of suffering. He even implies that Job and the prophets were in a happy condition while enduring their suffering. No child of God is ever really happy when out of the will of God.

It is of interest to note that the use of oil is but a symbol. James does not say the oil saves the sick, but that the prayer of faith does. Scripture often speaks of anointing with oil, especially in the Old Testament. In many of the ceremonies kings and priests were anointed with oil, signifying their consecration to office.

Whether the anointing spoken of in James 5:14 is of a spiritual and ceremonial nature or whether it is purely of a medical nature is not certain. The word here translated *anoint* may be understood to refer to the physical act of rubbing the body with olive oil, or it may refer to a mere application of oil with spiritual significance for the healing of the body. In either case, whether the therapy prescribed by James is spiritual or medical, there is no provision here for the gift of healing.

### John 14:12

> Verily, verily, I say unto you, He that believeth on me, the works that I do shall he do also; and greater works than these shall he do; because I go unto my Father.

Divine healers interpret the "greater works" to mean physical cures.

This passage gives us another great promise. Whatever healers may say to the contrary, it has no reference whatsoever to physical cures. No healer has ever been able to duplicate the healing ministry of Christ. Christ reached the climax of physical cures when He raised the dead. How can greater works be done? Can anything greater be done in the realm of the physical than to raise the dead?

If Christ did not have reference to physical cures, what did He have in mind when He said, "Greater works than these shall he do"? The Scripture itself answers the question it propounds: "And I will pray the Father, and he shall give you another Comforter, that he may abide with you for ever" (John 14:16). The record in Acts 5 reveals something of the fulfillment of this promise. The works which the disciples did were not greater in quality than the Lord's, but greater in quantity. Jesus explained the reason for this when He said, "Because I go. . . ." Thus the greater works are not greater because of more power, but because of Christ's absence from the earth.

Christ had just finished telling His disciples that His own words and works were the words and works of the Father (John 14:9, 10). If these greater works promised to the disciples refer to kind and not number, as healers claim, then the creature would be more powerful than the Creator. Furthermore, it is just not true in life that all followers of Christ do greater works than Christ, even quantitatively.

### Romans 8:11

> But if the Spirit of him that raised up Jesus from the dead dwell in you, he that raised up Christ from the dead shall also quicken your mortal bodies by his Spirit that dwelleth in you.

The greatest mystery that can happen to the child of God is the indwelling of the Holy Spirit. When divine healers flee to this verse as proof of their doctrine of healing, they are at that point admitting their confusion on the whole matter of the indwelling of the Holy Spirit in the believer. This great doctrine of the Word of God is the one major theme on which Pentecostalists and healers err from the truth. To misunderstand the doctrine of the Holy Spirit is to confuse every other doctrine with which He is associated.

Most of those who believe in the gift of healing today believe that the Holy Spirit comes into the believer at a time subsequent to salvation. Many verses of Scripture disprove this. Here are two: "In whom ye also trusted, after that ye heard the word of truth, the gospel of your salvation: in whom also after that ye believed, ye were sealed with that holy Spirit of promise" (Eph. 1:13). The believing and the sealing take place at the same time.

"Now if any man have not the Spirit of Christ, he is none of his" (Rom. 8:9). Here in the very immediate context of Romans 8:11 Paul says that absence of the Spirit means the absence of Christ. You cannot have one member of the Godhead without the others.

Many healers deny that Romans 8:11 refers to a future resurrection. Why they deny this is not known, unless to be able to use this verse as proof of a present physical restoration. Again, nothing in the verse or context says anything about physical healing or even implies it.

It will be granted that the words "shall also quicken" mean more than "raising from the dead," but that seems to be the emphasis here. The context of Romans 8:11 reveals that "the body is dead because of sin." In other words, our bodies have not yet been quickened; they do not have the effects of redemption in them. But there is the promise of redemption for our bodies. Verse 23 of the same chapter reveals our waiting for that redemption of our bodies. This redemption will come when Christ comes for His saints. Then shall these bodies of humiliation be changed (1 Cor. 15:51, 52). This becomes the answer to Paul's question in the seventh chapter of Romans, "Who shall deliver me from the body of this death?" (v. 24).

## THREE QUESTIONS EXAMINED

The real issue regarding divine healing and healers centers around three basic questions: (1) Did Christ die to provide immediate deliverance from sickness? (2) Is it always God's will to heal? (3) Is the gift of healing possessed by men today?

These are the deciding factors—not the other things that are usually brought into the discussion and which cloud the real issue. It must be acknowledged by all who accept the Bible as the inerrant Word of God that God has healed in the past and does heal now. Surely sickness is a consequence of the fall. Who would doubt that Christ healed or that He commissioned His disciples and the Seventy to heal?

The three questions mentioned above as those which constitute the crux of the matter regarding healing in the present day have been answered in this chapter in the negative. Our answer to all three of these questions is no, and we answer emphatically. Let us look at them individually and discover why we have answered the way we have.

**Christ did not die to provide immediate deliverance from sickness.** It is true that sickness and human suffering began when Adam sinned. Likewise, it is true that Christ's death provided deliverance from the guilt and penalty of our participation in Adam's sin. This includes deliverance from sin *and* suffering. However, while this twofold deliverance is assured and will surely be the possession of the believer, it is equally true that both are not received at the same time. The condemnation of sin is removed at the moment of faith in Christ (John 3:18), but the consequences of sin in physical suffering are never promised to be removed until the believer's body is transformed and glorified (Rev. 21:4).

The Scriptures bear abundant testimony to the fact of Christ's death as a substitution for man's sin, not for his sickness. Death and disease are a part of this life and will be until the curse is lifted. In the meantime we, along with all creation—and as a result of sin—groan and await the day of complete deliverance (Rom. 8:10, 21-23).

If healing is in the atonement in the sense in which healers claim it is, one ought never to use any form of medical aid to relieve physical suffering. To do so would be to accept deliverance from sickness on a different principle than deliverance from sin. We are saved by faith alone; thus if Christ died to give immediate deliverance from sickness as He did from sin, we ought to be healed by faith alone apart from any works, either on our part or on the part of doctors.

The body has built-in qualities to equip it to war against sickness; i.e., scarring of wounds, coagulation of blood, white corpuscles, etc. On the contrary, the soul of man has no such built-in qualities to equip it to war against sin. Rather, man is totally depraved, completely incapable of helping himself.

**It is not always God's will to heal.**     If God be God, He must be sovereign. Since all who are sick, even among those who are believers, and who pray for healing, are not healed, it is certain that it is not always God's will to heal. To insist that it is always God's will to heal is an affront against the sovereignty of God. God the Creator will not be thus browbeaten by man the creature.

The Bible simply does not teach that God is bound by His divine decree to bring physical deliverance to all men in this life. Evidence is abundant to the contrary. Finite man must never assume that he can thus impose upon the eternal and all-wise God. How dare the finite so order the infinite? As one hears those who claim to have the gift of divine healing on this matter, he is amazed at the audacity of the creature, mere speck of dust that he is, to so demand the Creator of the universe. Bernard Martin spoke for those who believe it is always God's will to heal when he said: ". . . Prayer for healing must be positive, a prayer from which all reserve and all 'ifs' must be excluded. It is a prayer relying on the will of the Lord, clearly expressed, and claiming the fulfillment of that promise."[2]

We only need to learn from the Savior what submission to the will of the Father meant to see the error of such reasoning. Jesus Christ was always totally surrendered to the will of His Father. He said so! If the Lord of glory found it necessary to recognize the will of God the Father all through His life to the very hour of His death when He cried, "Not my will, but thine, be done" (Luke 22:42), why should not we? Let us always remember, "The servant is not greater than his lord" (John 15:20).

**The gift of healing is not possessed by men today.**   This is true for the very same reason that the gift of tongues is not possessed today. Both of these gifts, and there were others, were sign-gifts given to the early church in the days of its infancy before the written revelation of God was complete. A sign-gift was a supernatural manifestation of the Holy Spirit given to convince the unbelievers of the authenticity of the message of the gospel and the messengers of the gospel. Thus, the initial purpose for the existence of the gift of healing is no longer present. Since God has not given us a new purpose for it, we may say the gift does not exist today. The previous chapter should be consulted for evidences of the temporary character of some of the gifts of the Spirit.

Furthermore, it seems clear from the emphasis upon the Church as the Body of Christ in Ephesians, and the absence of any mention of either the gift of tongues or the gift of healing in the listing of gifts in chapter 4, that these gifts were not given to the Church. The gifts listed in Ephesians 4 are gifts of men with God-given abilities to the Church. It seems more reasonable to believe that if Paul wanted the Ephesians to know that the gift of healing was a permanent gift given to the Church, he would have included it in the Ephesians 4 listing. Perhaps this is another indication that it was only a temporary gift given to men as individuals and not to the Church at large.

Along this same line we must be reminded that Christ healed and gave His disciples the power to heal, and they healed and even raised the dead. The Book of Acts records healings (at least nine of them); yet there is no command in any of the epistles to heal. In fact, the gift itself is only referred to once and that in a letter to a carnal and corrupt church (1 Cor. 12).

If men do not possess the gift of healing today, how are we to account for all the claims and demonstrations to the contrary? Divine healers are attracting thousands in this country and in other countries. Healing lines are visible on television. One can observe the healer and those who come to be healed as he demands God to heal, slams his hands on the person's body and screams "heal" or "demon depart," and then announces the cure.

It is easy to understand that when this type of thing is watched, and even participated in, experience determines doctrine and practice. How important it is to remember that the Word is our only rule for faith and practice and not the experiences of men, be they associated with a healer in this country or a heathen witch doctor in Africa.

With ready acknowledgment that God can and does heal, I believe the present claims of the healers and the healed must be categorized thusly:

*First*, some, perhaps many, people are healed not because a man possessed the gift of healing, but because God willed to heal and did so in spite of the methods employed by both parties.

*Second*, many who claim to be healed discover that the "healing" was not permanent. Evidently, in such cases the apparent cure was simply the result of mass suggestion, psychological shock and the power of mind over matter. This is very understandable since healers play upon the emotional and psychological powers of people to such a point that some lose all sense of reality.

*Third,* some "cures" may be accounted for on the basis of fraud. A great deal of skill is employed in handling healing lines. By carefully editing the healing section of the program, oftentimes the failures are omitted. This is deceit of the worst order and leaves the observer with the impression that all are healed when they are not.

The supersalesmanship of healers and the commercialization of the gospel, along with the deceit and deception, gives Satan an advantage to bring disrepute upon the Church of Christ. Too, many of those who were overtaken by the healers and who claimed healing only discover to their discouragement that the whole thing was unreal.

All too often a cure is claimed and advertised on the basis that the healed one feels better. Under such mass psychology and emotional pressure, who would not feel different? One would desire valid medical attestation of healing rather than the claims of the healer.

Only God can heal, and He does heal. He *must* not heal, nor does He always do so. However, claims for the gift of healing and the mass healing movement find no support in the Word of God.

NOTES:
1.  Kenneth S. Wuest, *First Peter in the Greek New Testament* (Grand Rapids: William B. Eerdmans, 1942), p. 70.
2.  Bernard Martin, *The Healing Ministry in the Church* (London: Lutterworth Press, 1960), p. 89.

# FOUR

# Current Trends

THUS FAR IN OUR STUDY we have observed God's sovereign method of distributing His abilities for service through the Spirit. Whatever abilities God's children possess, they are abilities which He has sovereignly and graciously bestowed. Too, it must always be kept in mind that these abilities are only to be used to exalt and bring glory to Christ. He is the unspeakable gift of God's love through Whom and for Whom all other gifts are given to man.

Two gifts which are being emphasized today were singled out for special attention. On the basis of the temporary nature and purpose of the gifts of tongues and healing, we have concluded, on scriptural authority, that these gifts are not among us today. Without denying their existence and practice in the apostolic church, we have noted that the gifts of tongues and healing are to be numbered among the other temporary gifts, such as the gift of prophecy.

While we affirm these truths, others in the religious world do not. This study would not be complete without some analysis of current trends. Specifically, we want to look at the development of neo-Pentecostalism and its relationship to ecumenism.

The modern ecumenical movement is receiving its greatest boost since its inception from what has come to be called neo-Pentecostalism or the Charismatic Renewal Movement. How can this be? Isn't the ecumenical movement liberal in theology and the charismatic movement made up mostly of evangelicals? What evidence is there that ecumenism is being advanced by neo-Pentecostalism?

Before addressing these and other questions, let's be sure we understand what is meant by neo-Pentecostalism and ecumenism.

## NEO-PENTECOSTALISM

Neo-Pentecostalism was born in an Episcopalian church, April 3, 1960, in Van Nuys, California. Soon after that, Pentecostal teachings began to spread rapidly in non-Pentecostal churches.

Of course, Pentecostalism existed long before 1960. Its rise is usually traced to January 1, 1901, when Agnes Ozman is said to have spoken in tongues as a result of actually seeking a baptism in the Holy Spirit and expecting to speak in tongues. Her experience took place in Topeka, Kansas, at the Bethel Bible College where she was a student. This was the beginning of classic Pentecostalism. From that time on Pentecostalists taught that believers were to seek the baptism of the Holy Spirit and that this baptism would be verified by speaking in tongues. The gift of healing was a vital part of the movement from the very beginning, as it still is.

> Starting in the 1920s and lasting through the 1950s, Pentecostalist spokesmen quarreled among themselves over the whole range of religious concerns: doctrine, church government, evangelistic techniques, finances, and cooperation with other denominations. So bitter did many of these disputes become that by the 20s

several large and many small Pentecostal denominations sprang up in all parts of the country.[1]

These quarrels and the splintering factions among
Pentecostals, as well as the common insistence that speaking in tongues was the evidence of the baptism of the
Holy Spirit, separated Pentecostals from the major Protestant denominations. Pentecostal churches and denominations grew, but they remained rather isolated from other
Christians.

But that scene changed in the early 1950s. Two na-
tionally organized programs were responsible for this: the
Full Gospel Business Men's Fellowship International and
the outreaches of Oral Roberts. Through these and other
similar efforts, Pentecostalism spread widely. But in spite
of the growth, there was still little visible effect upon
mainline American Protestantism.

The breakthrough came when the pastor of St. Mark's
Episcopal Church in Van Nuys, California, told his congregation he had received the baptism of the Spirit and
had spoken in tongues to prove it. It is not too much to
say that Bennett's announcement set into motion what is
now known as neo-Pentecostalism. Before long it began
to appear in all major Protestant denominations.

The spread of the classic Pentecostal doctrine of the
baptism of the Holy Spirit as distinct from salvation continues. Not all in the new movement, however, insist on
speaking in tongues as evidence of Spirit baptism. The
gift of healing (described in chapter 3) also continues to be
a major emphasis in neo-Pentecostalism.[2]

No longer is Pentecostalism confined to Pentecostal
and kindred denominations. It has, and continues, to in-
filtrate all of Protestantism. That is the major reason it is
called neo-Pentecostalism.

But that is not all. Neo-Pentecostalism has also entered
the Roman Catholic Church. It has not only entered; it has

made significant inroads. On April 8, 1967, the unbelievable happened. One who attended the now-famous Notre Dame prayer meeting described it like this:

> It was Saturday afternoon. I parked my car at the edge of the Notre Dame campus and walked to the administration building. Under its golden dome, Roman Catholic students were holding a Pentecostal prayer meeting. I did not know, as I opened the door of the administration building, that I was embarking on an adventure that was to extend across the world to hundreds of similar Roman Catholic prayer cells. I would visit monasteries, convents, churches and universities throughout the world, reporting on the growing Pentecostal movement.[3]

A historian quite sympathetic to neo-Pentecostalism gave this account of the distinguishing elements of the movement.

> 1. The new movement almost unanimously chooses to remain within it [sic] own denominational membership rather than joining established Pentecostal bodies (such as the Assemblies of God) or starting new groups.
> 2. With some exceptions most new Pentecostals do not require public speaking in tongues as proof of being baptized in the Holy Spirit.
> 3. A considerable number of the new group come from different social, economic, and educational groupings than the old. Most of the new come from upper-middle-class, well-educated backgrounds, being college graduates or college students.
> 4. The midweek prayer meeting is enthusiastically opened to anyone who wants to attend, regardless of any prior denominational affiliation.
> 5. Some new Pentecostalists have established communal living arrangements, sharing households and incomes.
> 6. All the new groups make their meetings as informal as possible concerning dress, prior planning of

the program itself, and remaining open to minister to the personal needs of any in attendance who ask for help.

7. The level of emotional expression is one of joy and celebration, but firmly controlled against excess display.

8. By contrast to the older Pentecostalism, which usually involved itself heavily in overseas missionary support, the new movement focuses primarily around the interests and needs of the local group. Those interested in missions show their support by working through their local congregation.

9. The new movement makes a more vigorous outreach to teen-agers and young adults.

10. The older moral code prohibiting any members from smoking, dancing, using make-up, and the like, is absent in the new Pentecostalism.

11. In today's movement many more women are actively involved as leaders.

12. Finally, the new Pentecostalists follow the established liturgical order when worshiping in their own congregations, rather than the older Pentecostal practice of spontaneous contributions at any given point. The new participants cultivate the "Spirit-led" services at their midweek meetings.[4]

## ECUMENISM

The word *ecumenical*, according to W. A. Visser 't Hooft, past General Secretary of the World Council of Churches, refers to "that quality or attitude which expresses the consciousness of and desire for Christian unity." The word at one time meant "pertaining to the whole earth." Later it came to mean "pertaining to the whole church." At the present time it is usually used to describe the desire for the union of all religious groups into one church. Thus as the term is used to describe the present movement within professing Christendom it means worldwide cooperation and fellowship among all religious bodies regardless of doctrinal agreement. "Unionism" was the term which was previously used to describe this attempt. The purposes and goals of those seeking church union have not changed; only the language used to describe their efforts has been altered.[5]

The modern ecumenical movement is made up of such organizations as the National Council of Churches of Christ in the U.S.A. and its global counterpart, the World Council of Churches. These and related ecumenical organizations are led by those who reject the cardinal doctrines of the historic Christian faith. Theological liberalism, not evangelicalism, characterizes these ecumenical organizations and the men who lead them.

True, some individuals in the churches which are supporting members of the National and World Councils of Churches are born again. Unfortunately, they stay in these churches and thus, often against their better knowledge, help to support efforts diametrically opposed to what they believe about Christ, the Living Word, and the Bible, the written Word of God.

## NEO-PENTECOSTALISM, AN AID TO ECUMENISM

At the beginning of this chapter I contended that neo-Pentecostalism was aiding and abetting the liberal ecumenical movement. Two questions are provoked by this bold assertion: What basis exists for such a conclusion? and Why is this true? How is it possible that a thoroughly liberal effort can be assisted by a movement made up mostly of those claiming to be evangelicals?

**What basis exists for such a conclusion?**    From statements made by those in the Charismatic Renewal Movement, their ecumenical intentions and desires are obvious. R. Douglas Wead, a sympathizer of Roman Catholic neo-Pentecostalism, wrote:

> Walls of theology that had separated Christians for centuries began to crumble in the wake of the most powerful Pentecostal renewal in sixty years. Lutherans,

Methodists, Episcopalians, Baptists and Roman Catholics were filled with a new enthusiasm for Christ—and they were fellowshiping together....

However, somewhere along the line we got confused. In the process of resisting overtures by the World Council of Churches and other modern movements (resistance I believe was correct) we made the mistake of thinking that unity itself was our enemy rather than compromise. This could be an error on our part. Being against the idea of unity is not only illogical, it's dangerously unscriptural.

Our isolation as Pentecostals has been a useful position.[6]

Erling Jorstad gave the following as one of his suggested guidelines for churches as they respond to neo-Pentecostalism: "Remember that like other new movements in church history, Neo-Pentecostalism may have a valid contribution to make to the ecumenical Church."[7]

Larry Christenson, who is appreciative of the charismatic renewal among Lutherans, made this revealing observation:

From the beginning, the charismatic renewal has had a strong ecumenical thrust. The ecumenical involvement has not been organizational, neither has it been superficial. It has been at the level of a common experience of the reality of the Spirit and the acknowledgment of the lordship of Christ. Denominational differences have not been wiped away, but a deep-felt sense of unity—one could almost say an obligation of unity—has continued to hover over the renewal. Seasoned observers of the ecumenical movement have singled out the charismatic renewal as the most vital and significant thing happening in the ecumenical scene today.[8]

More recent statements reflecting how neo-Pentecostalism is aiding ecumenism come from the 1977

Conference on Charismatic Renewal in the Christian Churches. The conference was held in the Arrowhead Stadium in Kansas City. The crowd was estimated to be 45,000.

It was a fully ecumenical five-day event organized by ten different charismatic fellowships. That meant it was really ten conferences in one, with meetings of Roman Catholics, Baptists, Lutherans, Presbyterians, Episcopalians, Methodists, Pentecostals, Mennonites, non-denominational Christians and Messianic Jewish Christians.

They represented an estimated 10 million charismatics in the United States—about 5 million of them Catholics and Protestants involved in "the renewal," and another five million in the traditional Pentecostal churches. . . .

The ecumenical aspect of the conference was unmistakable, as was the insistence by almost every major speaker on the importance of Christian unity. This was ecumenism springing from grassroots yearnings, successfully bridging gaps that councils and leaders have not been able to overcome. Father Francis MacNutt freely acknowledged before the huge stadium audience the indebtedness that he and other Catholic charismatics feel toward their Pentecostal and charismatic Protestant brothers for having pointed the way to renewal—and mentioned that today there is a flow of teaching and of understanding in the other direction as well.

Conference chairman Kevin Ranaghan showed a particular burden for advancing the cause of unity.

"The Holy Spirit has brought us together to say to us that in the renewal and through the renewal, there *will be* Christian unity," he said in his keynote message. He said he believed the conference was God's "living prophecy to the world that unity is a here-and-now reality, that it's growing by leaps and bounds, and that he has decided to have one people, one Bride. . . ."

Nelson Litwiller, veteran Mennonite leader and member of the Kansas City planning committee, said, "What the World Council of Churches, well-intentioned and godly people, could not do through restructuring, the Holy Spirit is doing today, of which the Kansas City conference is a very good example."

Vinson Synan, another member of the planning committee and general secretary of the Pentecostal-Holiness Church, commented concerning church unity, "The place to start is with common spirituality," and added, "This conference is a reflection of what already exists—unity on the grass-roots level."

David du Plessis said, "The charismatic movement will not change the world unless it is ecumenical, and it will not remain ecumenical unless it is charismatic."[9]

The question lingers, How is it possible for a movement composed mostly of those who claim to be evangelical to advance a cause so nonevangelical and unscriptural as that espoused by the ecumenical movement?

The answer to questions like these lies in a proper understanding of the nature of both neo-Pentecostalism and ecumenism. Both minimize doctrine and exalt experience. In the case of ecumenism, all the cardinal doctrines of the Christian faith are denied. Though the same doctrines are not usually denied by neo-Pentecostalism, they are minimized and are not made tests of fellowship. About the only major doctrines stressed by neo-Pentecostals are baptism in the Holy Spirit and the Lordship of Christ.

This lack of emphasis upon doctrine in both groups allows them to get together, to join hands in common cause, because their doctrinal differences no longer really matter. The important thing to them both is experience. To each group what one has experienced is far more important than what he believes.

Just at a time when the liberal ecumenical movement was running into some snags—both organizationally and on the grassroots level—neo-Pentecostalism came to its rescue. Intentionally or not, it is true: neo-Pentecostalism is providing ecumenism with a fantastic boost.

These current developments should cause us to affirm more forcefully our belief in the temporary nature of the gifts of tongues and healing. They should cause us to study more thoroughly the person and work of the Holy Spirit. And they should lead us to desire more earnestly the more excellent way, the way of love. To this more excellent way we now turn our attention.

NOTES:
1. Erling Jorstad, ed., *The Holy Spirit in Today's Church: A Handbook of the New Pentecostalism* (Nashville: Abingdon Press, 1973), p. 14.
2. Francis MacNutt, *Healings* (Notre Dame, IN: Ave Maria Press, 1974). MacNutt shows the relation of healing to the charismatic movement.
3. R. Douglas Wead, *Catholic Charismatics: Are They for Real?* (Carol Stream, IL: Creation House, 1973), p. 1.
4. Jorstad, *The Holy Spirit in Today's Church,* pp. 22, 23.
5. Robert P. Lightner, *Church Union: A Layman's Guide* (Schaumburg, IL: Regular Baptist Press, 1971), pp. 14, 15.
6. Wead, *Catholic Charismatics,* pp. 4, 65.
7. Jorstad, *The Holy Spirit in Today's Church,* p. 155.
8. Larry Christenson, *The Charismatic Renewal Among Lutherans: A Pastoral and Theological Perspective* (Minneapolis: Lutheran Charismatic Renewal Services, 1976), pp. 139, 140.
9. John Kenyon, "A Sign of Power and Hope," *Christian Herald* (October 1977), pp. 7, 8, 10.

# FIVE

# The More Excellent Way

THE WAY OF LOVE is the more excellent way. It is more excellent than any one of the gifts or all of them combined. It is more excellent because the love of which Paul speaks at the conclusion of his list of gifts in 1 Corinthians 13 is God's love given to men and demonstrated in their lives.

The thirteenth chapter of 1 Corinthians is a great treatise on love. Here the apostle is giving us his declaration concerning the greatest force in the universe—love. It is true that Plato and many others have written on love, but in this passage Paul surpasses all his predecessors, all his contemporaries, and all of his successors in this treatise *par excellence* on love. This treatise strikes the sweet and solemn note between the clang and the clatter of 1 Corinthians 12 and 14. I suggest that 1 Corinthians 13 is something like a rose in the midst of thorns. The necessity for the descriptions and explanations of gifts in chapters 12 and 14 arose because of pride and confusion in the Corinthian church. In direct contrast, chapter 13 is a hymn of love, a lyric of love, written by the most militant soldier of the cross who ever lived. Chapter 13 is an explanation of the more excellent way that Paul speaks of in the last verse of chapter 12: "But covet earnestly the best gifts: and yet shew I unto you a more excellent way." The entire thirteenth chapter is an explanation of the "more excellent way."

Paul is not merely attempting to show the Corinthians how to exercise spiritual gifts; he is also showing them the contrast between a life of gift-searching and a life of love-making. He is showing them a fork in the road—the way of gifts and the way of love—and Paul says the way of love is the "more excellent way." The world has degraded this chapter for the believer, and it has cheapened the love spoken of here, as well. Also, many have divorced the teaching of this chapter from the manifestation of the Spirit in the believer's life. This love of which Paul speaks so freely is not something which man gives to God; rather, it is God's love given to man by the Spirit of God. It is His love that is to be manifested in our lives and in our service. Therefore, it is not man's love for God but God's love in man.

The word for love here is a very forceful word. It is not the word for passionate affection or passionate desire; that word is never used in the New Testament. Neither is this the word for love which denotes mere affection. This is the strongest word that could be used by the apostle— *agape*. It is the love which God is. This is God's love manifested to men through the Holy Spirit, and worked out in the life as it is yielded to Him. Here is the greatest apostle of faith exalting love.

Of course, this is following in the steps of the Lord Jesus, for Jesus Christ Himself in John 13:34 said, "A new commandment I give unto you, That ye love one another. . . ." Peter expressed the same truth in 1 Peter 4:8 when he said, "And above all things [everything else] have fervent charity [love] among yourselves [one for another]. . . ." John said the same thing in 1 John 4:7 when he said in a pleading tone of voice, "Beloved, let us love one another: for love is of God. . . ." Let us love one another.

It cannot be emphasized too strongly that the love spoken of in 1 Corinthians is the fruit of the Spirit spoken of in Galatians 5:22. The singular number, "fruit," rather than "fruits," is pertinent. Paul does not say the *fruits* of the Spirit but the *fruit* of the Spirit, and the most important segment of the fruit is love: "But the fruit of the Spirit is love. . . ." The same word in the original appears here as in 1 Corinthians. And the difference between the fruit of the Spirit (singular) and the works (plural) of the flesh (Gal. 5:19-21) is love.

We want to study the more excellent way in 1 Corinthians 13 under three headings: the preeminence of love, the properties of love and the permanence of love.

## THE PREEMINENCE OF LOVE

This is given to us in the first three verses of the chapter. It has already been discovered that the apostle listed the various gifts in chapter 12. In chapter 14 he is going to deal with the actual manifestation of those gifts in the church. But here in chapter 13 Paul digresses a little bit. In his digression from his discussion of gifts, he shows us the importance of the place of love—the greatest force in the universe.

He begins this lyric on love by saying first of all that love is preeminent because it transcends spiritual gifts. Love goes beyond spiritual gifts in importance. He lists first of all the gift of tongues: "Though I speak with the tongues of men and of angels, and have not charity [love], I am become as sounding brass, or a tinkling cymbal." Paul's argument to the Corinthians is that the ability to speak a multitude of known human languages, even the language of angels, without love makes one's testimony worthless. You see, love is a universally understood language. It does not need an interpreter, and for this reason Paul says love is to be in the preeminent place, above the gift of tongues.

Love also transcends the gifts of mysteries, prophecy, knowledge and even faith (1 Cor. 13:2). In other words, the apostle Paul is telling us that even though he would have the gift of prophecy and would be able to communicate God's revelation to men; even though he may have a superior gift of wisdom and knowledge; and even though he may have mountain-removing faith, unless love is present—God's love manifested through him—he is nothing. One who is guilty of such misuse of God's gifts not only becomes nothing, but he is now nothing. So then love transcends spiritual gifts.

In verse 3 he tells us love transcends piety and martyrdom. "And though I bestow all my goods to feed the poor" (I may even be a socialite), "and though I give my body to be burned" (I may even be a martyr), "and have not love, it profiteth me nothing." Evidently it is possible to go the proverbial extra mile for one's neighbor and even to give one's own life without any gain or profit. No doubt some in this assembly were called upon to be martyrs, but Paul reminds them and us that more important than those things is the wonderful, wonderful gift of God's love.

The apostle places this same emphasis upon love in the other passages on gifts. The gifts of the Spirit in the New Testament come wrapped with love and grace. This is true especially in the 1 Corinthians passage. Directly in the middle of the admonition on grace gifts is this great treatise on love. It is also true in Romans 12. The apostle talks about the grace of God (v. 3); then he lists the gifts; and in verse 9 he speaks of the love of God. It is also true in Ephesians 4. Every gift of the Spirit is spoken of in a context of God's love and God's grace. Thus, without the love of God spread abroad in the heart every human effort is impaired. Now Paul does not say love will take the place of gifts, but he is saying that without the manifestation of God's love the exercise of the gift is of no avail. Paul portrays love, then, as preeminent above everything else.

## THE PROPERTIES OF LOVE

Perhaps as the Corinthians learned of the preeminence of love they said, "That's fine to talk about love as a preeminent thing, but what is this love? How does it manifest itself? What does it do? How does it relate to my life?" Paul gives fifteen properties of love in verses 4-7. As we list these, we must keep in mind that the apostle is talking about God's love. He is talking about divine love given to men by the Holy Spirit and worked out in everyday life. He first of all gives positive properties of love and then negative properties.

**Positive Properties.**    Notice the first positive property in verse 4: "Love suffereth long." That is to say, love is patient; love does not stand up for its own rights. This is a positive ministry of love, and it means that love brings restraint. Love is not quick to condemn; love is long-suffering. Now this is exactly what they were not doing in the Corinthian assembly because they were going to law with one another (1 Cor. 6). Paul says love does not do that. Love is patient; love suffereth long.

Verse 4 also says, "Love is kind." Love not only restrains, but it demonstrates kindness. Love has an active ministry; it overloads others with goodness. This is a lost art today—this matter of kindness. But the fact still remains that the love of God shed abroad in men's hearts, manifested by the Spirit, is kind.

Going on to verse 6, the last part of the verse, Paul

says love "rejoiceth in the truth." As a matter of fact, it rejoices in nothing but the truth. The Corinthians were rejoicing in human wisdom and in spiritual gifts. In the first chapter of this book Paul had to remind them of the danger of philosophical and intellectual wisdom. They were attempting to incorporate the wisdom of men with the gospel, and Paul had to remind them of something which we must never forget concerning the cross of Jesus Christ. No matter how beautifully it is talked about or how splendidly it is preached, it is always an offense to them that believe not; it is foolishness. There always has been and always will be a stigma to the cross. Therefore, Paul needed to remind these believers that love rejoices in truth, and truth is found in the Word of God.

In verse 7, "Love bears all things"; that is, love covers all things. This does not mean that love takes the ostrich approach, the stick-the-head-in-the-sand idea; but it does mean that love does not broadcast the sins and problems of others. Love is not quick to tell every secret of all the members of the Body of Christ. Love refrains; love boasts not; love is patient in that it gives every possible opportunity for reconciliation for another member of the Body.

Also in verse 7, "Love believes all things." This does not mean that love is gullible. Paul is not telling us that love accepts everything, but he is saying that love places confidence in other believers. Love does not act as a spy or a secret police or F.B.I. agent going around to spy on other believers. Rather, love uses the honor system. On the contrary the Corinthians were going around to see which clan the members belonged to. Some prided themselves as followers of Paul, others of Apollos and some of Christ. They were going around in the assembly trying to see who ate meat offered to idols and who did not. They were probably even going around the assembly checking on the women to see whether they wore hats to the assembly or not, or who spoke in tongues and who did not. How ridiculous! What a waste of time. Paul's point is that love does not do that; love believes; love trusts. Love makes room for differences, and love is kind.

The sixth positive property also appears in verse 7: "Love hopeth all things." That is to say, love does not despair; love does not give up; it is not pessimistic. In fact, the love of God is optimistic. The Corinthians needed this exhortation because they had lost all hope of ever seeing their loved ones (1 Cor. 15). Paul had to remind them that love hopeth all things. We, too, need this exhortation.

Finally, the last positive property: "Love endureth all things." Love perseveres; love has enduring characteristics. Paul is not speaking of the grin-and-bear-it attitude. He is saying, though, that love puts up with disagreements and differences; love does not divide over diversities; love does not cause splits in the assembly.

Following these positive properties, which are the things which love does, Paul gives the negative properties, the things which love does not do.

**Negative Properties.** Love is not jealous: "Love envieth not" (v. 4). It recognizes that others can make a contribution. It does not say, "Nobody can sing quite as I can sing; nobody can pray quite as I can pray; nobody can preach or speak quite as I can." Love does not do that; it is not jealous or envious.

In the same verse, "Love vaunteth not itself." Love is not boastful. The love of God shed abroad in the heart and out in the life does not change the family of God from a fellowship to a faction. Love is not a braggart; it is not boastful.

Also in the fourth verse, "Love is not puffed up."

Love is not proud. It does not stand in front of a self-constructed mirror. It stands rather in front of the mirror of God's holy revelation. The individual who is manifesting God's love does not harbor pride; neither does he manifest pride before others. The love of God produces humility.

The fourth negative property is in verse 5: "Love does not behave itself unseemly." That is, love is not rude or indiscreet. It could be paraphrased: Love does not act like the proverbial bull in the proverbial china shop. Love does not bulldoze its way through differences and disagreements irrespective of the feelings and viewpoints of others. Love acknowledges others. This strikes at the very heart of the Corinthian problem, for all through this epistle we learn that the Corinthian church was riddled through with problems. The heart of the problem was a lack of the manifestation of the love of God. No doubt this is the greatest problem in churches today.

Again, in the same verse, "Love does not seek its own." Love is not selfish; it is not self-centered. Love shows respect and consideration for others and to others. Love is careful in its use of the tongue. Did you know that the most ferocious monster in the world has his den just behind your teeth? This is a deadly poison. Martin Luther called it that little fire of hell and of joy.

Still another negative property appears in verse 5: "Love is not easily provoked." It does not become bitter or irritable; love is not hard to get along with.

Finally in verse 5, "Love thinketh no evil." It is not revengeful. Love does not keep a mental record of all the things that have been done against one, saying, "I will forgive you for this but not for that." Love does not do that; love is not revengeful.

The last negative property of love is stated in verse 6: "Love rejoiceth not in iniquity." That truth needs pondering. Love does not rejoice in the iniquity in the world, neither does it rejoice in the sin and iniquity that may come into the life of another member of the Body of Christ. Love does not step on another brother when he is down. Instead, the man showing forth God's love lends a helping hand.

Thus, within the compass of a few verses, Paul has told us what love is and does and what love is not and does not do.

## THE PERMANENCE OF LOVE

Paul deals with the lasting quality of love in verses 8-13. Love is permanent; other things will pass away but the love of God is eternal. In the first section (vv. 8-10) he compares love with spiritual gifts. Paul's reminder is that the gifts of tongues, prophecy, knowledge and faith shall vanish away. They will not last forever. On the contrary, the gift of love lasts forever. He illustrates this from human life in verses 11 and 12: When I was a child, I acted like one. When I became a man, I put away childish habits. The implication is that we are no more to expect the presence of temporary gifts today than we expect to see childhood habits in the life of an adult. During the immature days of childhood, things are done which are altogether out of place in the life of an adult. Paul is saying this to babes in the church who did the childish, immature things. Such things are expected of children but are not expected of grownups.

The exaltation of love follows: "And now abideth faith, hope, love, these three; but the greatest of these is love." God's love, my friends, is the greatest, the most powerful force in the universe, not only because it outlasts everything else but because it outranks all else.

Perhaps the most convicting exercise for the child of God is to place his name in place of the word *love* (or *charity*) in verses 4-7: John Jones is patient; John Jones is kind; etc. One cannot get very far along until he realizes the desperate need of falling on his knees before God and admitting his failure to manifest the love of God. Men see it as it is manifested by men. Let us not seek gifts or the praise of men, but let us rather seek to allow the love of God to manifest itself through us.

Our problem today is not understanding what gift we have or may not have; our problem is the manifestation of the love of God in our hearts and lives. The demonstration of the love of God is needed everywhere among believers today. What the Church of Jesus Christ needs more than anything else in the world is an immersion into the love of God. We need a baptism of love, a love that will manifest itself in our lives. Just as this was the answer for the discontentment and confusion in the church at Corinth, so it will be the answer to our problems if we walk in the more excellent way—the way of God's love. In the exercise of the many gifts which are present today, may we demonstrate God's love in us, since the fruit of the Spirit is love.

NOTE:
   I am greatly indebted for much of the material in this chapter to Arnold Ruler, *The Greatest of These Is Love* (Grand Rapids: William B. Eerdmans, 1958).